N.L. WALLACE

# THE RELATIONSHIP CURE

**The Ultimate Guide to Relationship Success,
Learn Relationship Advice on How to Improve
Your Relationship and Make it Lasts**

**Descrierea CIP a Bibliotecii Naţionale a României**
**N.L. WALLACE**
    THE RELATIONSHIP CURE. The Ultimate Guide to
Relationship Success, Learn Relationship Advice on How to
Improve Your Relationship and Make it Lasts / N.L. Wallace –
Bucharest: Editura My Ebook, 2021
    ISBN

N.L. WALLACE

# THE RELATIONSHIP CURE
**The Ultimate Guide to Relationship Success, Learn Relationship Advice on How to Improve Your Relationship and Make it Lasts**

My Ebook Publishing House
Bucharest, 2021

# TABLE OF CONTENTS

# CAN YOU REALLY STAY HAPPILY EVER

# AFTER IN A RELATIONSHIP?

Is it possible to live happily ever after? A good marriage is something you have to work at. Both partners have to be willing to work at it. You will need lots of tender loving care to keep your relationship fresh and exciting. When you are both willing to give and receive, the chance for survival of your relationship is increased.

**Tips for keeping your marriage strong and satisfying**

1. Whether you are just married or have been together for many years, in order to build a strong relationship you must learn how to communicate effectively. Listen to your partner and be sure you understand what they are trying to convey. Give each other your full attention when you are talking. Look at your

partner in the eyes when they are speaking to help you really understand them. Don't just hear. Acknowledge that what has been said is clearly understood.

2. Never assume you know how your partner feels about anything. Just because you like something don't volunteer them to do it with you. ASK! Always give them the courtesy to see if they want to do it.

3. Catch them doing something good. When your partner does something good, Say, I caught you! Then proceed to thank them for doing such a wonderful thing and tell them how much you appreciate it. You'll be surprised how far a little appreciation goes. When you make an effort to let your partner, know they made you happy you will find they will try to repeat doing kind things for the recognition.

4. Do something together every week that you both enjoy. Take classes together, go hiking, fishing, read poetry to each other. Find any interests that you can share and do these things often.

5. Be your partner's best friend. Cheer them on when they are working toward something they want. Hold their hand when they need it and give them a shoulder to cry on. Share dreams and goals and work together. Let them know you are proud of them when they accomplish goals.

6. Never neglect your partner. Don't get so wrapped up in your own life that you completely forget the everyday niceties. Kiss and hug them every day. Don't spend the whole weekend out with friends or watching TV. Make it a point to do something each weekend with your partner and you will grow closer together and have more in common to talk about.

7. "Never go to bed angry" sometimes this can be hard to do however, it is so important. Once you let an anger simmer for too long, it becomes much easier to come to a full boil and before you know it, you never work out any problems you just go to bed or leave the house to avoid them.

Learn to agree to disagree if need be to keep the peace. This will only work if you are totally honest about agreeing that it is ok to disagree at times especially if it is a minor problem. Don't waist time being angry about the small things?

8. It is OK to admit you are wrong. If you are wrong, admit it. Your pride will not keep you warm at night and a bad marriage is a high price to pay for it.

You can live together in harmony despite your individual differences. Practice these things and be sure to work out any fights before you go to bed.

Love and cherish each other. Build a strong bond by being loving and honest with each other.

# BUILDING TRUST TO BUILD A BETTER RELATIONSHIP

Are you honest with your partner? Are they honest with you? If you want to have, a healthy relationship is imperative that you are completely honest with each other.

Once you have caught, or have been caught in a lie is very difficult to trust each other.

When you trust each other, you will not need to wonder what the other one is doing when you are not together because you will know that they are trustworthy. Telling the truth helps maintain your faith in each other and strengthens your relationship. Without trust it is nearly impossible to have strong, loving, lasting relationships. So before you go and tell a lie to a partner, think twice.

When you are honest with your partner, you show them respect for their feelings. Honesty is the very foundation of any good relationship. By being true and honest you are expressing your love to your partner. Everyone deserves honesty.

## Follow these simple tips to build a strong relationship

1. Be honest about your job, the hours you work, your pay, and the people you work with. If you have a meeting with someone of the opposite sex, don't tell your partner you are working with someone else. You may think you are sparing their feelings of jealousy. However, if they find out, you were not truthful the first thing they will think is you are hiding something. You will at times have to work with others that your spouse could be jealously of, however if you have an honest relationship this would not be the case as you would have trust between you.

2. Do not tell your partner that you have the same dreams and goals if that is not the case. When they ask you to start working on them, you will become bored and resent doing it. Then if you blurt it out that you never wanted this anyway, how do you think they will feel?

3. If your partner asks you what's wrong, tell them and be honest. Don't say,

"Nothing" when it is, something. Tell your partner the truth and work it out. Unless you are open and honest about your needs and wants, how can they help you achieve them?

4. You should both be honest about how you feel about each others friends. If your partner has a friend which you, absolutely cannot stand, don't tell them you like them or you'll wind up doing things with them and resent it. Work it out so that when you go out with friends as a couple you go with the ones that you both like. When you go out alone with friends choose the one's your partner would rather not hang out with.

The best way to show respect for your partner is to be honest with them. After all if you can't be honest with them, who can you be honest with? Remember that being honest will build a strong foundation for a long and happy relationship.

# FIX YOUR RELATIONSHIP BY IMPROVING COMMUNICATION

### Communication Is Key

One of the things that becomes a source of problems for married couples is lack of communication. This is true especially of men, who are notorious for not expressing their feelings. A lot of arguments can be avoided simply by talking things out.

Couples should be open to each other about the problems and difficulties they are encountering. They should start communicating before it reaches a critical point and becomes a full blown fight.

Poor communication is one of the most common relationship problems that most people encounter. Good communication in a relationship necessitates a lot of skills, without which there is greater possibility of relationship problems arising. Starting with getting rid of all distractions such as TV's and radio noise, and arranging a quality time that suits both partners, is a good way to set off communication.

Do away with interrupting the other person when talking, and avoid categorizing the partner. Talking about good factors of the relationship as well as the relationship problems, can positively help create good communication.

Communication also involves non-verbal cues such as body language and with how common everyday things are done.

For example, when you see your partner crossing his arms while you're explaining something, he may not be receptive to what you are saying. Seeing his/her body tense up when you bring up a certain topic may mean that the particular subject is causing him/her stress.

A misconception people have over communication is that it requires words and a schedule to sit down and talk. While it is true that couples need to find time to talk on a regular basis, consistent communication goes beyond simply this.

The problem only comes when the other person fails to get the message – the problem of "miscommunication". A much greater concern than having either a good or a bad message is the other person to understand what you are trying to get at rather than ending up with the other's careless shrug of "whatever" – the worst form of bad relationship communication. Miscommunication is best resolved by asking. Do not make assumptions or jump to conclusions (that are most probably wrong).

Another obstacle to having a great relationship communication is communicating the truth. It already is a problem when a couple goes through with miscommunication, so what more if the sender expresses an erroneous message. Lying (or hiding the truth) always only makes things worse.

Finally, the last thing to keep in mind when it comes to relationship communication is how we communicate. If you're not sure of what the other is trying to communicate, then without hesitation, ask for an explanation, although you may get the frequent response of "don't you get it?!" Sincerely say, "I'm sorry, but I don't get what you're saying." And for the other, appreciate the gap-bridging; you would rather hear a question than a 'whatever'.

Don't finish your partners thought before they are expressed. In other words, if they say I was thinking about the back yard. Don't cut them off before they finish and say I already know what you want and I do not want to do it. Well the y very well, if given the chance may have said, I was thinking that what you suggested last week would be perfect.

By learning to listen to the needs of the other person and compromising, arguments can be avoided. Past issues should no longer be brought up, if at all possible, so that the couple can look ahead and face the future together.

It takes two people working together to make marriage work. It takes years and even decades to make it succeed. The direction of the marriage should always be decided by both parties.

# HAVE COMMON GOALS TO KEEP INTERESTED IN EACH OTHER

Before you ever get into, a serious relationship is advisable to talk about your dreams and goals for your life. In order to build a strong relationship you need to have things in common which are important to both of you. You both need to be totally honest with each other when sharing your goals and dreams or you will find yourself living with someone of which you have nothing in common to build on.

**Here are some important goals to talk about and compare**

1. Do you both have the same need for money and material possessions? If one of you is happy just getting by and the other has a strong desire for wealth, how will you achieve goals when your partner says, I don't see the point in working so

hard just to get more money. If you want your own business and they are not interested in building one with you, can you live with that?

2. How many children do you dream of having? What are your beliefs in raising them? What if you are unable to conceive of as a couple? Would you be willing to adopt? Are you ready for children or do you want to wait for several years after marriage to have them? These are questions that must be answered.

3. What do you believe in? Religion? Faith? A higher power? If your religious beliefs are different, it can make life difficult. What will you do when you have children? Which religion will you teach them? It is imperative to find someone that you can grow with and share beliefs and religious goals.

4. Do you dream of traveling the world or are you content to be a home body? Travelers and home bodies do not make great partners as one will always be forced to do what the other wants which will lead to resentments on both parts.

5. Each of you should right down your dreams and goals and then hand them to each other. By doing this you will not find yourself saying you want the same things they want just to keep the peace. Then look through them and see if you have any that coincide. Then if you do, great. Are they important to you? Do you have any goals that are identical? Build, on the ones you have in common. If you find you have absolutely no dreams or goals that are even close you may want to rethink the relationship before it gets too serious.

Follow the tips above to keep yourself from winding up with someone who in all possibilities you will both find yourselves in an unhappy marriage filled with disappointments and unrealized dreams for your life.

## SHOW APPRECIATION FOR YOUR PARTNER

Once you said, I Do, did the common everyday courtesies you used to offer and receive from your partner cease and desist? Do you feel like your partner simply expects you do things for him (her) and no longer believe you deserve to be asked please, and when you do it, to say, thank you?

One of the worst things you can do is simply forget about showing your partner respect and just expect. This is your life partner; don't you think you both deserve to be treated with every respect that strangers get every day from you?

A few years ago I was visiting a girl friend when her husband snapped, "Woman, get me a soda!" That alone shocked me, but what happened next was even more amazing. She jumped up and got it for him. In order to get respect from your partner you must expect it, and not allow them to treat you this way.

Now, I personally would have laughed at him for expecting me to get up and get him a soda when he asked for it this way. I would say. I don't think so. Have you ever heard the word please?

Give your partner respect, and expect it in return. How hard is it to use the same courtesy you used before you were married? These simple everyday courtesies should always be used when asking for anything from your partner.

"Please."

How hard would it have been to say, honey, I m so tired, can you please get me a soda?

"Thank You."

Once they bring it to you, a simple thanks or thank you will let them know you appreciate them.

And . . .

"You're welcome."

And when your partner says thank you. It is very simple to say your welcome back.

Your life's partner deserves to be treated with respect. You deserve to be treated with respect. These common courtesy words never go out of style. Use them every day and you will notice a lasting effect on your relationship.

Don't neglect your partner. You must give your partner your time and attention if you expect your relationship to grow and flourish. Married couples need constant reassurance from each other. Make an effort to accommodate your partner's emotional and physical needs.

**Notice things your partner does for you.**

If your partner does something around the house that you normally have to do then be sure to make a big deal about it. Say, thank you so much for doing that. I appreciate it so much. And give them a big hug and kiss.

**Spend quality time together**

Spend time talking, going for walks or start a hobby together. If you have nothing in common, the relationship can grow boring and you'll find yourselves off in separate rooms all the time to either avoid each other, or doing something you enjoy that they do not. Before you know it, you will be spending no time at all together.

Keep these tips in mind every day when you're with your partner. Add new ways to your list to show appreciation and you will find you can't wait to spend time together.

# SPEAK KINDLY, LISTEN, AND GROW YOUR RELATIONSHIP

Marriage is a partnership. If you want her marriage to be successful, you'll need to put your heart and soul into your relationship.

It is imperative in any long-term relationship to speak kindly to your partner. You also must be willing to listen with an open mind to your partners concerns. When you are speaking, talk in a clear and concise voice so your partner can understand what you are trying to stay.

Do not talk in circles or try to confuse your partner. In order for someone to understand what you are trying to say, it is very important that you only put across exactly what you want to say.

If you speak clearly, it will make it easier for the other person to understand exactly what you mean. Do not leave yourself open to be misunderstood. To start a conversation with your significant other, be sure they are listening. Sit in a comfortable position facing each other and look in each other's eyes.

You are now ready to start your conversation. Look your partner in the eye and tell them exactly what you want to say. If they are looking you back in the eye, they are most likely listening to what you are saying. Ask them to repeat back to you what you just said and what it means to them. This is an effective way to find out if they understand what you are trying to say.

Make sure that you are listening to them when they repeat what you just said. Once you are sure they understood you right, go on with the rest of what you wanted to say to them. Be sure to have them repeat everything back to you.

Listening is actually not a very simple skill. You will need to practice with an open mind. You cannot just listen, you must also try to hear and understand what your partner is trying to convey. Since everyone communicates differently, this can be very difficult at times.

When you are listening to the other person, do not be trying to think about what you are going to say next. Listen with your full attention. They deserve that from you, and you deserve the same when you are talking.

24

Practice speaking and listening with your partner. Set aside time every week to talk and listen to each other. Take turns, you can speak while your partner listens and then give them a chance to say what they want to say. Be sure to give them your full attention and they will return the same courtesy to you.

As long as you keep these simple tips in mind when having a conversation, you will be amazed at how much better you will understand each other and improve your relationship.

# 10 IDEAS TO SPICE THINGS UP IN THE ROMANCE DEPARTMENT

Is your love life getting a little (or a lot) dull?

Are you ready to just give up and live a life with no romance or excitement? You can add a lifetime of romance to your relationship.

STOP! Don't give up just yet. Here are 10 easy ways to heat things up again and add the very essence of romance.

1. Make this yummy massage oil and give each other a massage. Turn off the lights, light a dozen or so aromatherapy candles turn on some soft music and take turns giving each other a full body massage.

**Exotic Massage Oil**

2 fluid ounces of almond oil 16 drops Ylang Ylang essential oil 12 drops Geranium essential oil 10 drops Sandalwood essential oil 8 drops Patchouli essential oil 6 drops Clary Sage essential oil

Add essential oils to the bottle of almond oil, shake gently until thoroughly mixed.

2. Set out a bowl of grapes. Light some candles and turn on some soft music. Take turns feeding each other. This can be very romantic.

3. Dessert anyone? How about making a little dessert with your stomach as a bowl? Mix up some instant pudding and dish it out on your stomach then offer your partner some squeeze whip cream that they can add to their liking. No spoons needed for this dessert.

4. Give each other a good scalp massage or better yet take a nice bubble bath together using the recipe below, and shampoo

each others hair. While you're in the tub why not scrub each others bodies with the tropical body scrub recipe below.

This can be very romantic.

## Tropical Caribbean Dream Bubble Bath

3 drops rose fragrant or essential oil 2 drops jasmine fragrant or essential oil 1 ounce glycerin 1 ounce coconut oil 1 bar Castile soap (grated) 1 quart of water

Mix all ingredients together and store in a container. Pour into running bath water.

## Tropical Body Scrub

1 oz. Coconut Oil 1/2 cup sea salt 5-10 drops of Essential Oil of your choice Mix ingredients and slather over your skin rubbing in lightly to exfoliate.

5. Add some romance by pampering each other. Give each other a nice facial. Gently rub the facial on your partner's face with soft circular motions. If some of the facial mask makes it to other body parts, well, that could be fun too.

## Cucumber Apple Lime Facial Mask

1 egg white 1/2 cucumber, peeled 1/2 teaspoon lemon juice 1/2 teaspoon lime juice 1/2 teaspoon apple mint leaves 1 drop lime essential oil

Combine the first five ingredients in a food processor or blender and blend until smooth. Next add the essential oil and mix well. Refrigerate for a few minutes. Smooth on face and neck area and leave on for 20 minutes. Rinse well with warm water. This mask will stay fresh in the refrigerator for 1-2 days.

6. Give each other a foot massage using the Exotic Massage Oil recipe from tip #one.

7. Romance your partner by telling them how you feel. Make a list of things you love about your partner. Have them make one too. Then turn down the lights, light lots of candles and read your lists to each other.

8. Take turns tickling each others back. One night can be your turn and the next night can be your partner's turn.

9. Lay in bed together and snuggle, start behind your partner and tickle their stomach. Next flip over and let your partner tickle your stomach.

10. Lay down a shower curtain on your bed and pour aromatic body oil all over it and lay down together in the buff and slide around all over it together. You will not only have fun, but your skin will be silky and soft.

# 29 FUN TIPS TO ADD A LITTLE ROMANCE
## TO YOUR LIFE

Is the sizzle gone? Do you wonder if you'll ever feel that special feeling again? Are you ready to give it one more go? Great, you want romance? Check out these 29 tips to a more romantic life.

1.  Sit and turn all lights off. Light candles and listen to love songs and sing to each other.

2.  Write love notes to your partner and put them in places you know they will find them. i.e.; the medicine cabinet, the fridge, purse, wallet, inside laptop, briefcase, on the steering wheel in their car etc…

3.  Buy your partner a bunch of small gifts and then every time you catch them doing something right, give them one and say thanks for what they did.

4.  Dress up nice for your partner for no special reason.

5.  Buy her 11 roses, and then buy one artificial rose. When you give her the bouquet tell her that you'll love her until the last rose dies.

6.  Give your partner a head rub.

7.  Write a nice note telling your partner 10 things I love about you and put it on the mirror before they get up so it's one of the first things they see in the morning.

8.  Make an obscene phone call to them in the middle of the day.

9.  Compliment to your partner every day to improve your relationship. Tell them one nice thing every day. i.e.; your hair looks wonderful, you are so smart, and you make me so happy.

10. Take a bubble bath together and wash each other.

11. Do a couple of your partner chores for them so they will be more rested and more in the mood for romance.

12. Brush each others hair.

13. Put lotion on each other back.

14. Give each other a full body massage

15. When your partner comes home from a hard day, great them with soft music, candles and a fabulous dinner already set on the table.

16. Do a sexy dance for them.

17. When your partner get home surprise them by setting them down, taking off their shoes, and giving them a foot massage just because.

18. Snuggle up on the couch together under a warm cozy blanket and tickle each others stomachs.

19. Light scented candles all over the room to fill the air with your partner's favorite fragrance.

20. Feed each other chocolate or grapes while listening to soft music by candle light.

21. Go back to where you first met or had your first date and romance your partner with flowers and candles all over the place.

22. Spell out "I Love You" with Hershey's Kisses on the bed.

23. Have a pillow or tickle fight

24. Make a trail of rose petals from the front door to the bathroom. Have the tub running with bubbles and lot of aromatherapy candles burning with the lights out.

25. Take a 3 day weekend together at a spa and get pampered together.

26. Go up behind them and wrap your arms around their waist and nibbler on their neck.

27. Get a set of kid's water color finger paints and paint each other from head to toe in the shower.

28. Make arrows out of pennies leading to the bedroom where you have set up candle, champagne, and soft music.

29. Print this article and hang it on the fridge to give your partner ideas too.

Keep thinking of new ways to keep your romance alive. Your life will be more enjoyable for both of you. As long as you treat each other to special memories the flame will keep burning in your relationship.

Printed by Libri Plureos GmbH in Hamburg,
Germany

9 786069 838150